A Song For My Father

GW00500095

Also by **DESMOND EGAN**:

Midland (1972)
Leaves (1975)
Siege! (1977)
Woodcutter (1978)
Athlone? (1980)
Seeing Double (1983)
Snapdragon (1983)
Poems for Peace (1986)

Terre et Paix (French/English) (1988)
Echobogen (Dutch/English) (1989)

The Death of Metaphor (Prose) (1989)

DESMOND EGAN

A SONG FOR MY FATHER

for Tonia and Deirdre

up Athlone !

warm regards

Des

10.xi.89

1989
PETERLOO POETS

THE KAVANAGH PRESS LTD.

Published by

THE KAVANAGH PRESS Ltd., Newbridge Ireland
PETERLOO POETS, 2 Kelly Gardens Calstock Cornwall PL18 9SA

Poems © DESMOND EGAN

British Library Cataloguing in Publication Data
Egan, Desmond
  A Song for my Father
  I. Title
  821'.914

ISBN 1 - 871471 - 11 - 7:   Peterloo Poets
ISBN 1 - 870491 - 21 - 1:   Kavanagh Press Ltd.

Acknowledgements

The Irish Times (*Echo's Bones*); Radio Telefís Eireann (*Learning Russian*); *New York Quarterly* (*I chanced on a photo*); McCormack Centenary Committee, Washington (*Listening to John McCormack*); AFRI (*For Benjamin Moloise*; *Peace*); European Poetry Festival (*Dunnes Store Sale*); *Japan Daily News* (*Hiroshima*); Struga Poetry Festival, Yugoslavia (*Self Portrait With Typewriter*); *Trapani Nuova*, Italy (*Sicily Sicily*); *2 Plus 2*, Switzerland (*Have Mercy On The Poet*); Amnesty International, Kilcullen Branch (*For Father Romano*); Ireland-Chile Association (*Brother Sister Chile*); Goldsmith Summer School (*At The Birthplace of Oliver Goldsmith*); *Hundsrose*, Munich (*Germany*); *Etudes Irlandaises* (*Kilbeggan Distillery*).

Front cover: John McCormack by Charles Cullen (1984)
Back cover: Photograph by Seamus Murphy (1989)

Printed in Great Britain

For
Samuel Beckett

our valiant necessary wanderer
to the edges of this interpreted world

with admiration and affection

CONTENTS

I:
PEOPLE

I have studied the science of goodbyes . . .
Osip Mandelstam*

*from *Tristia* trans. Brown and Merwin; *Selected Poems* (Penguin, London 1977)

YOUNG GIFTED — AND UNEMPLOYED

guilty of being unemployed we   *jobbb*
saunter abreast against   *polyp*
shopwindows the male male street   *afternoon*
arms folded like mothers   *job*
our chat as wilful as   *herm*
two earrings in one ear   *herm*
the denim of our youth   *loss*
swelling with a salmon thigh   *oh*
                                       jobbb

you'd hardly guess our secret   *androg*
if you hit on us down town   *C and I*
in a dole coffeeshop off Main Street   *polyp*
schoolgirls who have left school   *androg*
giggling at a fella chasing a   *herm*
wasp round our table   *androg*
that you should be so lucky!   *afternoon*
                                       loss

or gathered outside a disco in the lightfall   *loss*
of a glass hotel with army bouncers   *loss*
                                               exiled

or staring into the near distance   *at home*
while months pass in parents' voices   *job*
and interview queues for interviews   *polyp*
and photocopying C.V.s   *dole*
and hitching alone to the rainy city   *home*
and prelim courses like demo tapes   *job*
and weekend waitressing for tips   *why*
our wage a bottle of house wine   *why*
and parttiming at filling stations topping up *jobbbb*
middleaged Ireland's cars   *dole*
the one who goes to get the petrol stamps   *herm*

▶

the face in the booth as tyres mutter   *androg*
pissoff pissoff   *C and I*
    oh

we babysit Friday nights   *secure*
trying to read *Woman's Own* after the central   *job*
heating clicks off   *why*
Just one day at a time   *dole*
Sweet Jesus   *herm*
yes it can all turn Country-and-Irish   *hermmmm*
and sometimes we are only pillion passengers   *androg*
                            roaring›   *drog*
down the *B and B* roads   *drog*
and sometimes we can feel a   *drogggg*
Dallas weariness in our bones   *polyp*
    WHY

and something is starting to die   *aaaaaaannnnndroooooooggggg*
    joooooooooooooooooooooooobb
but never you mind! the morning's   *sssssssssssssssssssecuuurrrre*
                  ours   *secsecsecsecsecsecsecsecsecc*
we'll swing into it in a gear gang   *ah morning morning*
young young young one last time   *of a day that*
and sometimes unemployment's   *turned*
               another high   *out*
on which we float and don't give   *different*
                    a damn
about adults waiting with the washup

B and B: Bed and Breakfast houses, offering lodging
C and I: Country-and-Irish music, a rough beast, born middleaged
herm/androg: creatures of doubtful sex

ECHO'S BONES

(For Sam Beckett on his eightieth birthday)

what have we to do with this hotel
its glass and boutiques and revolving chrome
and black waiter looking for a tip?

where we are sitting again at *doubles* of coffee
conferring like exiles *between the years*
your voice as gently Dublin as Yeats's
and nimbler than hands fallen
like my father's into age

austere and kindly — a monk on his day out
ready to consider any topic for a change
even writers! Joyce and that death mask —
Auden's verse about which we share doubts —
meeting Patrick Kavanagh in Paris —
the fifteen minutes you sat *post-prandium*
when neither you nor Pound uttered a word —
the Paris exhibitions? one shrug
puts them further off than Ireland
(and who could imagine you anyway
stalking peering with a catalogue?)
Company with your own father's 'loved trusted face'
calling to you out of the Forty Foot waves . . .

Marijuana in Ballymahon — there's a poem for you!

►

and you still surprise me now as you
lean across the marble top with ravelled face
and blue eyes that make us responsible
to quote from *Watt* those lines
'of the empty heart
of the empty hands
of the dark mind stumbling
through barren lands . . .'

and my mind knots again in loneliness
and we are no longer in a coffee bar but somewhere
in the outer space of your words
that almost intolerable silence where
we must try to hang onto some kind of dignity
out in the blinding dark you never shirked

later an embrace and you step off firmly
into streets gone eighty years old
God bless now Desmond

— and you Sam our navigator our valiant necessary
wanderer to the edges of this interpreted world

God bless

LISTENING TO JOHN McCORMACK

like anything human music has
body as well as soul in it so
listening to him singing I hear not only
the pure lyric note that note

but with the exile's ear I can also
find our shared Athlone
a flash of the Shannon down Friary Hill
the streets the midland spires the faces the narrow
laneways into the heart

and feel his live words cutting through
the tragic gloom of what is past

recover briefly my parents this side of history
my mother sitting in a boat to her island schoolhouse
across the morning of Lough Ree
or my father in his Thirties cap
arm — I know it! — out the window as he drives
McCormack himself going whispering to his concert
with Archbishop Curley and The Blacksmith of Ballinalee

it strikes like light along the river
below the Mathew Hall the old Promenade

where his bronze looks homeward

FOR BENJAMIN MOLOISE
hanged in Pretoria, Friday 18th October 1985

Life springs from death; and from the graves of patriot
men and women spring living nations. (Padraic Pearse)

Moloise the world stands
to observe a silence for you
for your people

together we bow our head
around that stadium of suffering
your death now our bereavement your courage
our abhorrence of every repressor

of those who would attempt
to hide freedom in a cloud of teargas
to beat justice to its knees with the *sjambok*
to dangle Africa from a white noose
to bury in quicklime the poetry of youth

and the world's silence runs like blood
it fills their sad swimming pools
seeps into verandahs and through bricks
it hangs on their bullwire it
creeps across the vaults of gold

and deepens
it becomes a scream
it enters our conscience too
with the wood of your coffin the
soft weight Benjamin of your life
as we take turns shouldering your remains
mourning yes but inspired as well at seeing
the spirit being true to itself
an ideal brandished like a burning spear

▶

so that when they hanged you we all became black

the hangman peers and hides and looks at his list

we Irish could have warned him no grave
would go deep enough to hold you
no more than it held Pearse
no more than it can hold any patriot

and though they tried to get rid of you
in the early hours when the world was asleep
the fools!
they did not see your soul breaking over Africa
over the whole earth dawning behind their digging

Benjamin son of days

---

root-meaning in Hebrew of Benjamin: *son of days/son of light*

DUNNES STORE SALE

big business breathed its hot breath
on my neck as the four of us trolleyed-in
to the dodgems of this whole emporium alive with
preoccupied shoppers yellow-red posters fluorescent
avenues of movers stoppers choosers replacers
mammies without with daddies carrying children
babies in buggies amazed (like me) at the scene
young ones in gear pretending not to notice
stray bargain males
7 p.m. on a Thursday night and all Newbridge
seems to have had the same bright idea
how the hell did I let myself in for this?
10p off marked price
special offer
SALE SALE SALE THE ONE YOU'VE BEEN WAITING FOR
while the sheer quantity of goods moves towards a
quiddity as tantalising as barbecued chickens
making things seem possible teasing our greed into
creeping slyly out between the aisles
going surreal with the jumble of choices:
nappie liners Rioja toothpaste or extra-virgin olive oil?
someone behind the scenes knows
a thing or two about us and speaks from time to time
through an oracle whose utterances cut into
margarine music . . . *was 20.99 now 9.99*
(two women shoot one another a look
they would never waste on a man)
and remember customers . . .
a microcosm with a micro-point of view
more coherent I began to think than my philosophics

looking into a piled trolley ah
was like looking into someone's fridge
it gave the game away we   ➤

had got as far as the English queue at the checkouts
where registers bipped and plastic bags filled
up like Santa's when all of a sudden
the scores of squares of wattage down the hangar bli
nked failed without further notice
OUT!
dumping us humans among the lines of shelves
our fingers loosening on the 50p handles *wha-*
that apocalyptic second for which
no one (as always) was quite prepared
everyone everything shoppers assistants goods
plunging reduced

and is death a little like that?

COMING BACK ON A MAY EVENING

I put the boot down into summer
an idea on instead of the radio
and growing like modern philosophy on wheels

when a flotilla of cloud anchored
below Moate scattered it all glinting
in an eight o'clock sundown

a drifty smoky curtain on the passenger side
tore into shower into light while the edge
of the whole world brightened up as if with that
desperate hope of *l'homme moyen sensuel*

and the scene began to turn into a mood

whose brown mists fell down Kilbeggan
down Garryduff boreen where my mother came from
and on the stone ruins on the briary lane
of many young sundays

as everywhere opened up in creation's rain
splattering flooding on the windscreen
a wholeness that began to shelter me
from the wrong kind of seriousness

sink not
the
rope
of
thought
into

the
bottomless

well

---

right column: Camus

THE RAILWAY STATION
(For Viv.)

we head there in a rush
taking the dead backstreets
and end up waiting together on
that old stone platform

time gusts around the walls
and down the empty tracks

which soon fill with noise with energy
lighted carriages a brief intimacy of faces
resigned as the station master's

the hurried goodbye —
a late traveller bending to the ticket window —
two girls plonking across the bridge —
the slap of doors the ticking delay —
this station is every one I was ever in

you hop on I lift *the pair* to wave
as you move behind others through the compartments
get settled in a place near us before
all those lights and lives slowly
smooth off on diesel fade into the mind

leaving that heartbreaking quiet
the posters for holidays
the shuttered booth

HIROSHIMA

(For Akira Yasukawa)

Hiroshima your shadow burns
into the granite of history

preserves for us pilgrims
a wide serious space
where one may weep in silence

I carry in my mind
a glass bullet lodged deep
the memory of that epicentre where
one hundred thousand souls
fused at an instant

and the picture of a soldier
tenderly offering a cup of water
to a burnt child who cannot respond

the delicate paper cranes

---

paper cranes: folded paper birds left at the Children's Monument by children from all over the world

LEARNING RUSSIAN

ever since my soul began growing up
part of it has been learning Russian
the part that knows about winters
the serious part

Mother Russia! despite your goosestep dogma
your tanks trundling across the cobblestones of Europe
betrayed by that great bald mind you
remain for me a peasant in a homemade shawl
offering bread and salt and a place by the hearth

you adopted me orphaned by youth
and gave me Dostoievsky for a big brother
to influence me more than an affair of the heart
he put manners on me changed me quietened me for keeps

you gave me Akhmatova we walked along the Neva
by sombre gardens with covered statues
sat talking on our seat by the Fontanka canal
and her words still follow like sad eyes
keeping me late for everything

Tsvetayeva too both present and far away
makes me phonecalls since she took me in hand
with the sad intensity of an older sister
who knows too much

you gave me poor Mandelstam
oiling his hair at the mirror until
suffering came to take him into custody
and he trudged like Keats into that other country
whose longing speaks straight to the heart

►

Vladimir Mayakovsky too became a pal
uneasy with energy drinking too much of the future
infuriating friends put out like a dog
and in-between eyeing that stage revolver
with the one real bullet in its chamber

how many times have I shouted down the years
at him at Marina at Yesenin no
not to make ink of their blood not
to give death a hand?

oh and Russia your music! its
unmistakable steppes of vastness unable
to shirk the tragic cold
it rages round the rooms of my student days
more nourishing than any studies I now realise
like the films the few which beat their way through science
towards that *zone* where black and white might at last
burst into full colour into the gold-skied
ikons of longing

Rubyleff Tarkovsky Solzhenitsyn Rachmaninoff Zamyatin . . .
yes so many of your family shared what they had with me
in the hungry years and since they took me in hand I
can still feel that grip like a foreign accent

Holy Mother Russia thank you
for having taught me your language

---

zone: cf. *The Stalker*, a film by Andrei Tarkovsky

SELF-PORTRAIT WITH TYPEWRITER

in the polished steel I trap a face
its writer's droops its expression of flesh
almost too intimate even for me yet
wary as a Chinese sage's
the hill hollows I needn't go into
not to mention a mouth turning like Shaw's
up one side down the other . . .

funny business this
pulling one's chair to a desk of nights of years
able to achieve little of what I feel and yet
fingering at the keys in hopes to touch
something humbly out of the everything
while cheeks begin to sag like breasts
en el fonda del corazon tristeza

tristeza que es amor

if only I could shuck off this obsession
this need to scribble day in day out
you have no idea of the nuclear energy I
could transmit in every direction
the villages of easy difficult things I
could electrify laughing

not a hope though

and I understand perfectly well
why my friend the Emperor Hin Tsung
attended to his calligraphy his painting
as the dead hordes were carving up his kingdom

Machado quotation: *In the depths of the heart a sadness/sadness which is love*

SKYLARK

(To the memory of Kieran Collins)

so Kieran old pal your fingering of
the most plaintive music
has been interrupted for keeps the whistle has
slid to the floor in this senseless
exposing silence
and no one else can ever
coax from it your tunes

you have walked out the door
the leather jacket the black western hair
taken for granted with that
precise diffident point of view the shy half laugh
just gone   only this time
you will never slip back join us in a corner and
produce when the mood ripens from your breast pocket
a couple of *penny whistles* no never
play again play play
head to one side out of the way
of the life dancing round the lounge

in notes from the Burren edge the
spirit notes we cannot fully follow
the music beneath the music
tragic hopeful our race moving again in a way in your
spirals knotty interlacings loops and purls of feeling
a skylark over the Irish bogs one
unknowable last time

➤

and now old friend we are left with the pause
to clap when it's too late to call after you
the thanks that never got said to stand in respect
at the true music of what has become your life
sweet as a spring well

put away the whistle I don't want to hear
in death forever my brother I'm saying goodbye

The Skylark: Collins is recognised by musicians as having made this tune his own

SICILY SICILY

through the mists around Aphrodite's mountain
a lookout I'm told could sight the Carthaginian
longships cutting out from Libya
and that's the way I'm cupping my hands now to
catch Sicily a glimpse of you

knowing that what lodges in travelling always includes
off-centre things: Thucydides in a traffic jam
the smell of Marsala an actor's gravy voice as much as
that vast bay of Siracusa beyond imagination
coldblue murderous
where the triremes had thumped and smashed and
drowned slowly like men
dragging down the Athenian dream partly our own
to break the surface again in history's flotsam
with Nikias' last speech

and only the sound of a wave away I can hear
the chatter of tourists turning Greek translating into
thousands of soldier sailors moaning dying
in limestone mines too hot then too cold
where caverns dripped despair and beneath overhangs
the shadows were *corpses heaped on one another*

yes Sicily black Palermo of no music
where there are mountains there is harshness
and the seas all islanders know must foam with tragedy
sure as the Doric skyline of Selinunte

but then we each lug about our happiness unhappiness
and you were only mixing-in your own
with the faces the lives that pass on a path
with the laughs the *che bella*s for infant Kate   ➤

with Scammaca chained to his glasses dentures whistling in zeal
with Nina and Pietro smiling from the distance of language
with Enzo in short sleeves lugging like a talisman
his translator's briefcase through the punic heat
or with a twinkle-eyed grannie dressed like a nun
who hadn't to hide behind books

memory! a scent of oleander the shirt sticking to my back
tyres screeching down the black mafia streets
the lift door to our *pension* slapping in the darkness

after the reading we sip beer at 2 a.m. in a lobby
and I know that time is already refining crude experience
and will leave a signature indelibly like Euainetos'

so since it's unlikely I'll make it back again
that's how I'll carry you Sicily in my wallet:
a silver tetradrachm with dolphins leaping
around your Arethusa head

Libya: The Greek name for Africa
Euainetos, greatest of the coin-makers, put his signature to his coins

KILBEGGAN DISTILLERY

(For Frank Abbott who reopened it for us)

somehow it's the bloom of the weirs
that first whispers *fugit inreparabile tempus*
even before the foursquare chimney stalk with
LOCKE'S
which rose on so many Sunday afternoons I
even recall the snake-tongued conductor on top
and the bricking within stone the wall clamps the
crúiskín sign above the entrance it's all
only a little more faded now than when we were
young

but look! the gentle tumble of the millrace
is turning for us again that high high wheel
lifting its wooden tongues dropping fringe upon
fringe of
lacewater gracile as First Communion veils

and though it's true the gates open nowadays into
an empty courtyard full of silences
that the vats store only a sodden gloom
or show their ribs like burial ships to newcomers
that engineering is rusting back into iron
abandoned with fluorescent offices
and the bell on the gallery no longer rings quitting
for bosses maltsters coopers labourers all
made redundant by the years

yet light continues through those attic windows
absorbs the dark varnishes worn pine floors
and brings like the spill of water new energies
for all who wish to rebuild and preserve
their own sweet past

whitewater
rushing
over
flowing
falling
falling
falling
splashing
foaming
churning
tossing
foaming
moving
moving
broadening
becoming
continuum
changing
into
years
years
the
years

▶

and the distillery intimates mysteries which can
touch us nourish us with time's peculiar art
the malt you can almost smell! a worker's name
carved in a beam a century ago

and outside in old trees old sunshine by the same
                                        old river
our mill turns metaphor

---

fugit . . . Time flies, irretrievable (Virgil, *Georgics*)
crúiskín: jar (of whiskey)

FOR FATHER ROMANO ON HIS
45th BIRTHDAY

in you Romano I salute the few
who hand out like bread to others
their ordinary life
and build up block by block
anonymous in the loneliest villages
their chapel to the spirit

who bear witness in remote marketplaces
wearing white against the sun
who make their flesh and blood an angelus
pealing across huts and plots

deeper than bull horn or gunfire
than any saluting officers who imagine they
can bundle truth into a jeep
and stub out freedom with cigarette butts
and build walls higher than the sky
and riddle with foreign rifles
the soul they think they have blindfolded

in you Romano I salute every
missionary of hope
especially if I may the unsung Irish
the ones who have scattered themselves like seed
across forgotten worlds

and when I hear that such as they as you
have ended up in prisons or ditches
I feel as well as rage a fierce pride a
joy of sorts at this reminder
that the resurrection continues

►

Romano your persecutors will only succeed
in squeezing from your body the blood of Christ
and though they dump you in one compound or another
your soul flies with ease up over
their pathetic cement their money sentries
their rusting barbed wire

flies across the globe makes people like us your family
who would otherwise never have known you

and in your name we join hands
fall into step and sing together
the song of your life

no one can stop our march

Fr. Rudy Romano, a Filipino priest, 'disappeared' in 1985 during the last months
of the Marcos regime. He had fearlessly tried to organise poor *campesinos* into
demanding living wages and tolerable work-contracts. Witnesses saw him being
forced into an army jeep.

PARIS 1985

somewhere beyond comforting a tiny tot
was standing by a stairway in the world
of a department store where I waited

her eyes waiting too
not crying any longer as the shoppers
busied over and back she paid no heed
to the supervisor holding one stray hand

lost for evermore just then a
small planet of solitude
somewhere of abandonment and love no
outsider could hope to reach
loneliness entering her very being
and not a thing we could do

so soon

we delayed
as helpless as she
en attendant

suddenly there came a rush down the steps her
mother her big sister!
she was running she was swooped up
into a whole embrace
the women crying now

and I moved off about my no-business
walking by the counters
yes I admit it hiding a tear

remembering my father

Frère Jacques
Frère Jacques
Dormez vous?
Dormez vous?
Sonnez les matines!
Sonnez les matines!
Ding ding dong
Ding ding dong

LISTENING

(In memory of Bill Evans)

his reaching piano fingers
his paleness the glasses
the submissive listening head

*it's love
this time it's
love*

will sink no more into chords

he has slipped out unsmiling
through the drinks the night talk the barmaids
before the end of this final set
at 51 to die

*my
foolish
heart*

the group plays on

and already his records sound older
fraught as last wishes

waltz for Debbie

or words remembered
from anyone's life if
we had the ear

is that what his knuckles were
straining to reach? the only
notes which might be

Evans, a noted Jazz pianist, often played the popular 50's song *My Foolish Heart*

BROTHER SISTER CHILE

we Irish men and Irish women reach
out to you our thoughts our fing
ers the light river of our hands and
                            hands
until they touch you like the gift of
                            tears

we send you this flaming bread
this food which no khaki mouth can
                            gobble

they have cut off your music at the
                            wrist
use ours! we will sing for you the deep
undying anthem of freedom

they have gagged your voice
take ours instead we
will speak for you will cry
across the world at your agony
will scream out for the beaten the
prisoners in kennel cells the lives
lined up against walls of blood

we will mourn for the dead for
families that have become our families
will rummage with you for the
                            disappeared
will howl with anger at the torturers at
the money monsters from nowhere

listen and you will hear our sound

?Que les pasa a las calles traga-
                            gentes de repente?
Calles antropofagas se han
                            vuelto de repente
estas vulgares, rectas calles
                            afeitades cada hora
con la crema azul del smog de
                            cada dia.
De repente
son calles espadachines de la
                            muerte,
largos caminos directos a las
                            celdas;
nadie sabe si sabe su destino.
De repente
solo la calle sabe

What has happened to the
                            streets?
the people-swallowing streets
                            so suddenly
have they turned into cannibal
                            streets
these ordinary straight roads
that were groomed always
                            with
the blue hairoil the smog of
                            everyday
suddenly
they are bullying streets
                            streets of death
those streets

➤

both old and young enough to echo   *streeeeeeeeets*
                            echo   *streeeeeeeeeee*
even in the maw of curfew streets   *eeeeeeeeeeeeeeee*
look carefully and you will see a line   *eeeeeeeeeeeeeeeeeeeeeeee*
                          of light
round the copper door of the prison
          they have made of Chile

our love like a patch of sky

wrist: a popular songwriter/guitarist had his right hand cut off, after the fall of
Allende, 1973
?Que les pasa . . . from a contemporary Chilean poem, published under the
pseudonym Teresa de Jesus (Curbstone Press, U.S.A. 1979)

PEACE

(For Seán MacBride)

just to go for a walk out the road
just that
under the deep trees
which whisper of peace

to break the bread of words
with someone passing
just that
four of us round a pram
and baby fingers asleep

just to join the harmony
the fields the blue everyday hills
the puddles of daylight and

you might hear a pheasant
echo through the woods
or plover may waver by
as the evening poises with a blackbird
on its table of hedge
just that
and here and there a gate
a bungalow's bright window
the smell of woodsmoke of lives

just that!

but Sweet Christ that
is more than most of mankind can afford
with the globe still plaited in its own
crown of thorns

➤

too many starving eyes
too many ancient children
squatting among flies
too many stockpiles of fear
too many dog jails too many generals
too many under torture by the impotent
screaming into the air we breathe

too many dreams stuck in money jams
too many mountains of butter selfishness
too many poor drowning in the streets
too many shantytowns on the outskirts of life

too many of us not sure what we want
so that we try to feed a habit for everything
until the ego puppets the militaries
mirror our own warring face

too little peace

HAVE MERCY ON THE POET

(Tengen piedad para el poeta – Neruda)

— the poet waiting his turn at the Bank Manager's confessional
Lord, have mercy
— the poet hands in trousers in a garage
Christ, have mercy
— the poet filling-in his Tax life
Lord, have mercy
— the poet at the aluminium entrance to the supermarket
Christ, have mercy
— the poet opening one more envelope of verses
Lord, have mercy
— the poet hemming and hawing to friends' questions
Christ, have mercy
— the poet haranguing an audience of 17
Lord, have mercy
— the poet *holding down a steady job*
Christ, have mercy
— the poet pausing at the bestsellers rack
Lord, have mercy
— the poet in a student's pullover
Christ, have mercy
— the poet exaggerating his indifference
Lord, have mercy
— the poet tearing life into the wastepaper basket
Christ, have mercy
— the poet scrounging down the jewelled road
Lord, have mercy
Christ, have mercy

AT THE BIRTHPLACE OF
OLIVER GOLDSMITH

Here, as I take my solitary rounds
Amidst thy tangling walks and ruined grounds
And, many a year elapsed, return to view
Where once the cottage stood, the hawthorn grew,
Remembrance wakes with all her busy train,
Swells at my breast, and turns the past to pain. *

Goldsmith we're here both old and young
many of us from those same places you
uncovered first like silver in a bog we have collected
to stand today around your flame

and if *look!* you unexpectedly too
came strolling down that 18th. Century laneway
a bit late even by Abbeyshrule time
to stand on the fringe of our crowd
we'd deck who it was I think as we would
a half neighbour from a parish across the ways

naturally you'd be careless about your appearance
(we of *the centre* have our priorities)
your face more obviously Irish than ours
not puffed with hormones never pasteurised
not weakened on the likes of
chocolate telly and newspaper attitudes

— more of a peasant's look or maybe I should say
a country fella's (my father's category)
rooted and physical — well *midland*
not without that hint of the complacent we
still have to guard against ➤

---

*from Goldsmith's *The Deserted Village*

yes and I think we'd hear even in your quick talk
our very drawl in which there are no mountains only
rivers of raincloud slowing along
through low fields where the cattle graze but
ready like yours to laugh

I bet you never lost that accent
no more than you bothered to explain yourself to
Boswell and the literary crew
a to hell with it feck it what's the differ?

furthermore if you did join us this June afternoon
you'd be *Ollie* in no time on first name terms
after a session in *The Rustic Inn* unlike many
Irish writers with English minds

but *lookit* Goldsmith I knew you well anyhow
having bumped into you as you did into Carolan
on my way to Tang School with my mother

and often enough those days I walked
in spirit round your house
put back the roof cleared it cleaned it
told the honeysuckle to bloom and the bluebells
sat down at the hearth with your brother Henry
whose death made you go searching for
Auburn in Springfield Essex
to find it in your own heart

oh my mind still slows-down beyond Farrells
at the sharp corner of your *hawthorn bush*
— no road will ever bypass that for me
nor the *busy mill* paddling on unseen
across the lush meadows of childhood
nor Kilkenny West with *the decent church*
familiar and strange as tea from the flask
each picking at consciousness like the *Three Jolly Pigeons*
over McCormack's closed bar

➤

all the unnoticing trips to my mother's school
when I would wander outside time the only time we
really learn anything about anything enough
to feed on it for keeps
when imagination comes out shyly moves
like a leatherjacket in the tree where we played
outside that two-storey slated presence
its map and double desks the swing blackboard upstairs
which frightened me like sums in a Kerry accent

strangely enough Goldsmith the drive home
was into a different mood how can I explain
the sense of loneliness the heartbreaking disconnection
which seemed to grow with the long curving wall at Auburn
a shudder abandoned in the fields?
some inland sombreness we share with you
like the line of our hills?

anyhow we're here to pay tribute
not just to you Oliver don't get a swelled head
but to poetry to
the lark above the meadow this minute

to the lasting human things

and today especially to your memory
acknowledging in our oblique manner that
we have been fed by you changed
in ways subtle as pronunciation

that in your modest fashion you helped us take courage
to be ourselves the only way: to recognise
our whitethorn in blossom all across June
the yellow flaggers that labour not
the pathos of our landscape
love in a forget-me-not

►

so if you're up there having a yarn with
Kavanagh and Ledwidge and maybe even our fathers
talking greyhounds and characters and who lives where
the eternally significant
we doff to you the caps we aren't wearing
and here where you were born one of us
twine our thoughts into a living wreath
to leave when we have gone

DARAUF

although it's June the ring
on my backdoor feels cool as a
                        coffin's

and there's movement against the
                        ditch a
sizzle on the flat roof ah

rain slinks around the glass kitchen
beading on a pane as I shave runs
glugs sweetly into the gutters by
the last of the flowers

where our blackbird forages peeks in
cheeky as on that night while
droplets go sliding colourless form
little lakes on the folding table
where we ate where the glass held
                        sunset
where you were
your hands your
silver fingers

*where the retinae focus intently
they will see the object even
                        afterwards
and an amputated limb I'm told
twinges occasionally*

*that's how you
linger*

words

GERMANY

Germany when I think of you these times I
don't just have a flash of
divine Schubert peering from steel glasses
Der Gipfel des Berges of Heine's Rhine
my roommates Lovis Corinth and Broch or
Emil Nolde who knew about the demons
those blue infinites of Altdorfer where space
                                    becomes time . . .

now what I catch this moment scrambling all other
                                                signals
is that cursed wall
its lights its cement guards its turrets of neo gothic
its bodies its camp wire tight as strings tuned
on iron stays through your soul

we from a two flag island know
something about plantation and borders and
                                    armed patrols
around the unapproved roads to wholeness and
empire's pig eyes beckoning
OUR COUNTRY NEEDS YOU
flicking over natives like forms to be filled and
                                            stamped
frowning down long dispirited queues
of cars of people of years we have learned that
politics is mostly impotence in drag
leaving the spirit spreadeagled for another search

Hörst du
die
Nachtigallen
schlagen?

Ach!
sie
flehen
dich

Mit der Töne
süssen Klagen
Flehen
sie
für
mich

ein

einszwei

einszwei
einszwei
einszwei
einszwei
einszwei
einszwei
einszwei

➤

while barriers grow high as hatred throbbing   *einszwei*
                              continually   *einszwei*
almost inaudible as a Thor freezer   *einszwei*
yes we have developed an ear for that sound its   *einszwei*
subliminal hum through seven   *einszwei*
centuries   *einszwei*
we're seven hundred years ahead of you there   *einszwei*
had grown well used to it before Bismarck riveted
                              you together

                                                      einszwei
seven hundred years the sadder for it and   *einszwei*
nothing to offer except a car bomb

FEED THE WORLD

Geldof if all your efforts
all the phonecalls the meetings the smoke
of energies blasting through loudspeakers all
the stadiums amplified with youth

the great cry which lifted that night like a bird
to hover over Ethiopia

— if all that had helped to save one human being
one infant barely able to suffer
one mother averting her head . . .

it would have been worthwhile

and to how many did you give the kiss of life?

but more than that you did more
than transport hope to the famine-stricken
(which no one shipped to us in Black '47)
— for the first time since Cain did the dirt
you came the nearest I know to gathering the world
however briefly back into one

one family of man flickering like a picture cutting
in from some other channel
how could you guess how far your
loaves and fishes would go?
or that you would help us rediscover
something lost down memory?
break our apartheids?

and as no one lives on bread alone
feed us who are also starving?

II:
SEQUENCE: A SONG FOR MY FATHER

What we have really grasped cannot be expressed in any way at all, and cannot be transmitted to anyone else, not even to oneself, so that we die without knowing the exact nature of our own secret.

E.M. Cioran, *Drawn and Quartered*
(translation © Seaver Books, New York, 1983)

I.

I chanced on a photo

my father in shirtsleeves
standing by the greenhouse

on so relaxed a summer's day
no one bothered to pose
least of all the dandelions

and my mother saying something to Kate
who wonders with the yellow roses

the privet hedge we cut down since looks lovely
a doll lies forever in the sun

and I can almost smell the dinner
see our folding chairs and table the
other side of my camera

the red serviettes blowing

II.

the heart monitor	*out of the exile of age I*
jigged up	*rediscovered him as you do your youth*
down	
its small screen	*we got closer than ever*
	thick as thieves

➤

American Wake: party held before someone took the emigrant's ship to America
almost never to return

50

we were afraid
to look
and not to

his life jerked along
out of control now

zig zagged through
all conversation

as that graph
plotted everyone's
utter fragility

until
Wednesday 17 April
20 past 9 it
thinned
out

gave one last kick
before
nurse switched it off

until it came his turn to leave
after the American Wake of
those last years

and when time was up
I would sit by the locker
holding that hand

gone gaunt now sunken as his eyes
and blotchy from needles from suffering
but soft and warm as I always loved
and vulnerable as his father's hands
protecting him in a Communion portrait
still hanging near the desk and books
in my old room

III.

awake when the clock radio went off
I heard a voice singing
'Sé mo laoch mo ghile m'fhear . . .

and in that instant just there I re
alised it how valiant his life its shape
now almost completed

mo laoch
m'fhear

feeling
has its
tributaries

can run
underground

or sometimes
like the Shannon

►

'Sé mo laoch . . . : He's my champion, my hope, my man from the Irish poem.

that utterly tender moment when you see
someone very close to you as a stranger:
                              someone
standing at the door as your car moves
away and away down the metaphysical street

and the same day at Ballinderry Hospital
in the intensive care unit where he lay dying   *flood*
for the first time since I put on long trousers I   *its*
kissed my father   *banks*

IV.

that morning in intensive care
light falling from April across the quietness
of two other empty beds their curtains

as we talked about early days he
began for no reason to weep
great shuddering male sobs
to himself

my father! it was nearly as shocking
as that black blood
4.30 a.m. the morning he went

Daddie—

and even yet
even this wet windy August day I want
to throw my arms around you shield you

I who have no shield

V.

no more season tickets
produced like blue gold from *the little*
                                                    room
no more fixture lists
on which he filled-in scores

no more following him out
on a rushed lunch and expectancy
no more parking at the galvanised gates
after his impatience had jumped

no more coming up afterwards to where
he waits frail and grinning by my car
a home win! *they were steeped!*

no more nosing through the roadful of
                                                    fans
radio hoarse with other results
my father letting down the window to
old cronies absorbed back into the crowd

no more sundays

the crook of my arm under
his shoulder-pit gone gaunt
unnoticed as the years
                    clocking up

in tandem with Sister

knees up that's it Tom
1-2-3-lift!

briefly I get the weight
of his whole life

grand! *he would always say*
                    grand
trying to take over again

o fix the pillows

VI.

I am four and from the kitchen stairs
I can see him through the dark shop
at the path his window down say
ing something to my mother

I cannot get there in time
be swooped up and out
in a wide dizzy swing

run
oh run

tired bodies
glimpsed passing
on the ground floor

humiliated by
our need to suffer

dying air

and in the lounge
worn suits   ▶

53

my word still chases

as he begins to move

worn faces
too intent on
some television game

one asking time and again
When is the News?

VII.

the night he died he
was pulling wearily at the quilt
speech gone on a tray

I thought it
would be easy
to die

we too had nothing to say
nothing left to offer
but wait grip his hands

it's
not so easy

had it come to that?

look Des
(I had dropped a syllable)
I can't even
cod myself now

everything turned so simple
all our complexities our
story hopes imagination message
simpler than I ever knew

the night nurse tightening bedclothes
leaned down to ask *is there*
anything you want Tom?

was this husky shadow
over the phone
this familiar turned stranger

all that was left?

a fan! I barely caught his last words
the bottom of that old humour
its irony partly mocking himself
Athlone to the bitter end

this
as much as the stuff which soon oozed
of its own out of his patient mouth
finishing any last chance
broke me

does still

►

VIII.

I'll go on ahead
and he does now

on a *dander* down past Walsh's
tipping his public cap
stopping at people not shops
hey Ginger — across to some red-
               headed hopeful
on Doc Martin's side of the road

still ahead of my running words
ah Des is it yourself!

go easy a minute Pop

dinner finished
he has left the table and
hatching in the newspaper chair
has folded his hands touching
               thumbs
turned his head to make a smart
               remark
and clicked his heels laughing
               on us

while the kettle boils

IX.

I threw down into the glaury sticky grave
one daffodil from the spring of 1985

tossed it out from me saw it
bump against a freshly dug wall

and with it part of myself
my youth the good times and middling since
the matches the trips to Dublin
deals the shop our walks at *The Bay*
agreements disagreements many and many a laugh
christmases and gatherings and our last weeks
a dying hand

the wet clay of our jumbled loving past

I never saw it land
                                ➤

---

glaury: from Irish 'glár' — watery mud

X.

no flat tire: he knew a thing or two
but my father I'm happy to say was no intellectual
he read the papers beginning with sport
and that's about it

so *an ordinary fella* like him wouldn't want to head
down any avenue of Paradise with the likes of
Aquinas Eriugena Simone Weil Nietzsche . . . my friends
figuring things out no
not his cup of tea *at all at all*

neither would be make a beeline for poets' corner
— in spite of his respect for whatever was *tops*
even in *wheelbarrow racing* — so
Shakespeare Pessoa Akhmatova Machado and co
could jaw away for all he cared

and I have to admit he'd also *give a miss*
to Emmet and Tone and Padraic Pearse
Parnell Davitt Dev Bobby Sands and the others: a
situation I personally don't have to enjoy
but like it or lump it he was himself
and politics didn't really fit

nor music either though he'd give a wave
to John McCormack whom he knew

nope he'd walk by all their groves in Elysium
to the spot where *Kerrigan* Joe O'Meara Tommie Kilroy
Artie Brock Dan Maher Jim Higgins Pakie and the others
were drinking tea chatting about Athone

or go for a stroll with Muscles and Dinny Hannon
talking football

▶

XI.

week he died I planted a shrub
one flowering currant in the lawn
opposite our front door
rooted it deep
into the earth of 1985

hoped it
might make some other April
                    blossom
say *Take it easy you cod you*
cheer and challenge

like his laugh

a widow woman *asked him as*
                    a favour
to try and lay hands on some bit
                    of marble
for her husband's gravestone

no better man! a slab off an old
                    washstand
now holds the inscription
up in Clonown among the crosses
                    and stones
the dead rich and poor
thin as plywood funny and
                    touching
it seems almost to bend with the
wind across the bog

her own name has gone on since
and when I look
I can see my father's

XII.

that day I brought him back from Mullingar
turned out our final trip

he and I the old firm
on the very road he had driven me
with my mother and my new suitcase
to St. Finian's College

now I was in the driver's seat
our journey running and running
with reminders with landmarks with memories with fields
with years the years dropping
freshly behind in road . . .

▶

57

each of us knowing too much we simply
in best Irish fashion talked about people
and he laughed deep at Loughanavalley passing
the gravestone erected by a priest before he died
See you later on the bottom

the kind of crazy gent my father lapped-up!

he kept chuckling at it that Sunday afternoon
my car moving through the bare ditches of February

heading home

XIII.

and already it seems an age
since we chatted in the sunlit ward
since I held his hand
and kissed his cold forehead
as all that he was faded away

leaving the whole show less real

— there's no kick anymore in finding
a place full of antiques *at the right price*

and who gives a curse if Athlone Town
win lose or draw in the Cup
or Clarke play a blinder against Rovers
or Dundalk sign up
Michael O'Connor during the off-season?

it hardly matters if I get a good review
or a talk of mine repeats on radio

he's not around to make them news
by the way he'd register

▶

58

Georgetown University have bought my mss.
people react with a variation of *o really*
lacking love's imagination ah

only now when things have gone a bit *off*
do I appreciate that zest of his

how can I bring myself ever again
to watch a home match?

XIV.

memory damp paperbag   *only a word*
lets things drop out unnoticed day
by day by new day   *an*

lookit it doesn't matter a curse   *outward sign*

I think of you all in one *go*
you are joking at me over something   *the spring bell*
some statement we both know I didn't quite make
the laugh's on me the irony   *jangling*

that's o.k. Pop   *on the shop door*

XV.

couple of weekends afterwards I
made that heart-sinking turn again

and up the drive to the entrance
which felt different already without my mother's
yellow rusty Toyota in place

climbed the questioning staircase stepped
down that landing of unhealthy light
into the corridor the bittersweet
gripping my bagful of thanks   ➤

beside the Unit our room lay open
empty as the wardrobe

I looked out its window at the fields
the cattle indifferent as before
the cloud houses where other lives were lived
a familiar knifeblade of lake
and the end of the daffodils beside
the road to the world

everything
pretending to be

XVI.

month's mind: a small group
along the top two pews of an empty church

and in the epistle Gallio a pro-consul
tells the Jews hounding Paul to feck off
mind their own bleddy business
tough customer the type
that always amused my father

our remnant goes up home

and as we pour tea and try to act normal he
sits to the table his usual place
says *no tomatoes for me*

only he doesn't

we have been
transubstantiated into the past

and even the past is dying

XVII.

Cornamagh

living avenues of gravel
leading here
leading there

someone in the distance

the box hedge trimmed
and beeches in a whisper
as when he brought me down
to see this plot

a street of shadows
going to his sunken grave
our bouquets stripped to wire

and leaves like years
lodged in the sodden grass

*I do not weep with my mother
standing at McKenna's monument*

*only his poor tired body
lies here under the trees
only his shaggy eyebrows and white
hair
his eyes no longer curious
the lip he would clench at us
exactly as my small daughter does
his hands that gave the game away*

my father is elsewhere

XVIII.

Epitaph

Tom Egan does not lie here

not the warmth of his little finger
not his laugh that was full of life
not his spirit that saluted from the door
into the street the years

nor our love more lasting than granite